PET OWNER'S GUIDE TO THE
CHIPMUNK

Chris Henwood

DEDICATION

This book is dedicated to Ian Norman 1960 – 1997.
Greatly missed.

ACKNOWLEDGMENTS

During the writing of this book and my years of owning chipmunks, I have had help, information, stock and a lot more from a number of people. To these I would like to extend my thanks, especially to Mole, Michael Boddington, Sue Field and Tony Atkinson.

PHOTOGRAPHY

AMANDA BULBECK

Published by Ringpress Books Limited,
PO Box 8, Lydney, Gloucestershire,
GL15 6YD, United Kingdom.

First published 1998
©1998 Ringpress Books Limited. All rights reserved

ISBN 1 86054 068 6

Printed in Hong Kong

ABOUT THE AUTHOR

Chris Henwood has been keeping and breeding small animals for over twenty-five years. During this time he has been responsible for introducing several species and mutations to the pet fancy. He is an international judge of hamsters of all species, and is the author of numerous books and articles on all aspects of small animals and their care. He acts as an advisor to television programmes and to the RSPCA on small animal care. He keeps a varied collection of species at his West Sussex home which ranges from chipmunks and hamsters to a Shar Pei dog.

CONTENTS

1 Introducing The Chipmunk

It is now quite a few years since I obtained my first chipmunk, and I have been hooked on them ever since. The chipmunk is not a common pet at present, but it is a very appealing animal and is increasing in popularity. It seems that the more people see them, the more people want to own one. Indeed, very many people do find that, once they own and breed chipmunks, they find it very difficult to part with the babies. I speak from experience!

This book will give you all the information you need to help you decide if the chipmunk is the pet for you and your family. It should give you a good idea of exactly what is involved in the care of chipmunks, and I hope it will also be a useful source of information for people who already have these beautiful creatures in their family.

WHAT IS A CHIPMUNK?

The chipmunk is a small burrowing rodent, a type of ground squirrel, full of curiosity, very active, and an excellent climber and escape artist.

The chipmunk is a gnawing animal, and, in common with all rodents, it has two pairs of chisel-like incisors, which grow throughout its life. The outer surface is coated with hard, yellowish enamel and, by grinding the teeth together, the animal keeps them very sharp.

The two chisel-like incisors grow throughout a chipmunk's life.

The chipmunk is lively and inquisitive – and it is a great escape artist!

Chipmunks do not have canines, and the space between the sharp incisors and the premolars enables the animal to draw its lips together when gnawing and thus to prevent indigestible fragments from entering its mouth.

Chipmunks are agile climbers, with curved claws and ankles which turn through 180 degrees. This allows them to climb very effectively, and yet they are also excellent burrowers. You should bear all these points in mind while making the decision about whether the chipmunk will be a suitable pet for you and your family.

Although there are many species and sub-species of chipmunk in the wild, at present there is only one species widely retained in captivity. This is the Siberian chipmunk (Eutamias Sibiricus). As a rough guide to size, it is a little bit bigger than a Syrian hamster and smaller than a Fancy rat, but with a bushy tail. It reaches from 80 to 160 mm in

length, and the tail is about the same length again.

ORIGINS

In the wild, the Siberian chipmunk has a very wide range, extending from North European Russia, across Siberia to China, Korea, to the Kurile Islands and finally to Hokkaido in Japan. In this huge area, there are thought to be approximately nine different races and subspecies of chipmunk. The most commonly seen subspecies in captivity is from Korea, although there are some people who feel that the Cinnamon (see Chapter Five: Breeding Chimpunks) is of the 'Hokkaido' subspecies.

There are now also a few colonies of wild Siberian chipmunks in Germany, Austria, France and elsewhere, all of which

This is the commonly seen sub species Eutamias sibiricus lineatus from Korea.

The dilute coat mutation of Eutamias sibiricus lineatus.

are the result of pets escaping. I should point out that in the UK it is illegal to allow a pet to escape and to establish itself in the wild.

SUBSPECIES

Most of the Siberian chipmunks in the UK are from Korea. Many different authorities have different opinions about whether the species should be categorised into the various different subspecies detailed below. Little study has been made of the chipmunk, except for that performed by the scientists and field biologists of the former USSR. The

information given below results from their work over the years. I have not listed in detail how the subspecies differ, because many of the differences have to do with teeth and width of the stripes, and you would probably need to be a real expert to understand why some are regarded as different to others – it certainly confuses me! I hope that you find them interesting, but be warned that, if you try to find some of the locations on a recent map, some of the names may now be different since the break-up of the USSR.

In the wild, chipmunks prefer areas of pine forest with underbrush.

EUTAMIAS SIBIRICUS SIBIRICUS: Central Siberian chipmunk. Found in Central Bashkiria, the pine forests of the Tomsk and Yeniseik areas, south to the upper reaches of the Amur and the Kirin region of Manchuria. It is very similar to the West Siberian chipmunk, but the black stripes are broader, and the buttocks tend to have a pinkish/cinnamon tinge.

EUTAMIAS SIBIRICUS STRIAUS: The West Siberian or European chipmunk, found from Vologda in the west to the lower regions of the Kama. It does not pass to the right bank of the Kama, but runs to the Urals and Tobolsk. Its colour lacks the reddish rust, and the black stripes are rather narrow.

Survival means always being on the alert.

EUTAMIAS SIBIRICUS ORIENTALIS: Found in the southern part of the Maritime territory, the Ussuri and Manchuria. Its colour is very rich and very reddish.

EUTAMIAS SIBIRICUS LINEATUS: The species that we regard as the Siberian chipmunk, it occurs from the Korean peninsula and the islands of Yezo, Sakhalin and Hokkaido.

LIFE IN THE WILD

In the wild, the chipmunk is naturally a more timid animal than it is in captivity, but it is

EUTAMIAS SIBIRICUS JACUTENSIS: The Yakut chipmunk. This subspecies' range includes the wide area from Khatanga and Vilyui to Penzhina in the east. It is reported to have the narrowest stripes and the palest colour.

The burrow will be fiercely defended.

Wild chipmunks dig a series of galleries within the burrow.

item, such as a nut or a berry.

They seem to prefer areas of pine forests, with underbrush and low bushes, beside field and river valleys. They rarely appear to climb higher than four metres from the ground, and they tend to be rather solitary animals, living in loose colonies with overlapping home ranges. The females have smaller ranges than the males. These ranges centre on the single entrance to the chipmunk's burrow, and this is fiercely defended by its owner. Should another chipmunk approach, it will be chased away. However, as the chased animal approaches its own burrow, the tables will be turned and the chased animal will turn and chase the original chaser away. Thus, the chase will go to and fro until one of the animals gives up.

When danger approaches, such as a man at a distance, the chipmunk will whistle jerkily and keep still for quite a long time. During this period, it will rise on its hind legs and carefully watch the source of danger. If a human walks very slowly and quietly, without any sudden movements, it is quite likely that he will be able to approach to within fifteen or twenty steps of the animal. The

not regarded as too cautious, and so can easily be observed. It runs rapidly, but is much more at home in windfall branches than it is in fully mature trees. It is a very good climber and can easily jump between branches 5-7 metres apart, and can change direction mid-air with the help of its tail. Some of these jumps resemble the jumps of flying squirrels, with their outstretched legs. Chipmunks are also fond of hanging by their hind legs in order to reach some tasty food chipmunk will then rush away, giving repeated whistles. Naturally, the more contact an individual chipmunk has with humans, the closer the approach it will allow. Frightened chipmunks do not always run to their burrows – they usually hide in the branches in dense foliage.

BURROWS

In Siberia, chipmunks usually dig their burrows in roots or under fallen trees – rarely in live trees. Sometimes, there are whole chipmunk towns in screes. Some of the burrows found begin in a rotten tree trunk and continue deep underground. It can be difficult to find the entrance, as they are usually concealed by overhanging vegetation or by stones or roots. Chipmunks have two different types of burrow systems. One is a simple tunnel and nest chamber, used as a temporary home, and the other is an extensive system with various side galleries and chambers for storing food, a latrine and nest chamber, with a bed of moss grasses and shredded leaves, etc. The depth of the burrow will depend on the type of soil, and may well vary from 40-95 cm and be up to four metres long.

When excavating its burrow, the chipmunk digs a work tunnel, which is marked by a pile of soil on the surface. On completion, this is closed and the entrance is opened from underneath, so that there are no signs to show the burrow entrance. The burrow proper will be well hidden under rocks or windfall logs or among tree roots, and a chipmunk fleeing from some form of danger will rarely run straight to its burrow,

Like hamsters, chipmunks hoard food.

like a ground squirrel, but will hide elsewhere.

In a dug burrow the entrance is either round or oval and no more than 4 cm wide. The first part of the burrow descends from the opening at an angle of 45 to 70 degrees. After two or three bends the burrow ends in a nest chamber, and two or three side galleries branch from the main burrow. Some of these are used only as a toilet. The main burrow will often widen in one area, and this will be used for storage. Alternatively, the chipmunk may dig a side burrow for this. The nest chamber is usually 60 to 70 cm below ground.

FOOD

Chipmunks are mainly vegetarian in the wild, as in captivity. Animal foods do not appear to be an important part of its diet, but will be taken if available. The remains of bank voles have been found in chipmunk nests, as have small nesting birds, although the chipmunk rarely appears to eat eggs. The most common animal foods are mainly snails, ants and other small insects.

From studies of chipmunks in the wild, it has been found that only 0.3 per cent of the diet is made up of the seeds of cultivated plants, although in areas where millet is grown, this may form a higher percentage. According to these studies, the food of the wild chipmunk falls into two groups. The first group includes trees and shrubs such as hazel, maple, linden, bird cherry, raspberry and honeysuckle. The second group consists of seasonal plants, berries and seeds of forest plants such as strawberry, bilberry, bramble, wild rose, sedge and wild grasses, oxalis, crowberry, aconite and spindle tree.

If these foods are scarce, then the chipmunk will eat cultivated foods – wheat, rye barley, buckwheat, oats, corn, flax, millet, sunflower, apples, pears, apricots and cherries have all been recorded.

Providing that there is an adequate food supply, the chipmunk will remain in the same area all of its life, although, when the food supply fails, Siberian chipmunks have been recorded as migrating to new areas. Like the hamster, the chipmunk is a hoarder, and non-perishable foods such as seeds, berries and nuts are collected all year and stored in the burrow, while some will also be buried within the individual's home range, away from the burrow.

As with their larger relatives, the true squirrels, such as our own non-native but very familiar grey squirrel, chipmunks tend to hoard more in the late summer and autumn when they are getting ready for the winter. Food is moved to the burrow in their cheek pouches. Chipmunks rely on these food stores to see them through the winter months, when they tend to remain underground. In the winter, in some areas, chipmunks hibernate, but this is not a continuous hibernation and tends to only last for a few days at a time. On a warm day in winter, chipmunks will come to the surface and sunbathe.

In the spring, the males emerge first and, on the appearance of the females, the annual breeding

Seek expert advice before choosing a chipmunk as a pet.

season will take place. A female will find a prominent place above ground and call to the males. Little has been written about chipmunks' courtship in the wild, so I shall leave breeding information until a later chapter.

CHOOSING YOUR PET

My animals are pets first and foremost, and the fact that they breed is 'icing on the cake'. The breeding animals usually stay with me for the whole of their lives. However, people who breed chipmunks for profit may well dispose of their stock as it gets older. The breeding age of a female may extend into her sixth year and beyond, but, on occasion, some females become infertile by their fourth year. Males will continue to breed throughout their lives, providing the female is willing and a younger rival is not present. So how can you tell that an animal is older?

The older normal and cinnamon chipmunks may lose some pigmentation to the coat, taking on a greying appearance or even losing some of the fur. This is not so easy to detect in older dilutes.

As chipmunks become more popular, they become easier to obtain. However, they are more

Colour, age, and tameness will affect how much you pay for your chipmunk.

popular in some areas of the country than in others. Added to this, breeding results are better in some years than in others, and so you may find it easy to obtain an animal one year, and very difficult the next. You can expect a shortage of animals to affect the price, as does the colour, age and level of tameness of an animal.

You may well find that your local pet shop either stocks chipmunks or is able to obtain animals. Ask where the animals came from. You may discover that they were commercially bred, which means that they will either have been bred in large aviaries or small cages, and are unlikely to have had much contact with humans. While these animals will undoubtedly make good breeding stock, they may not make good pets – they will take a while to tame, and some may not become tame at all.

You may be able to obtain your pet from a small breeder or someone with a single pair of animals. Chipmunks bred in this way will be more used to interaction with humans than those commercially bred. Small breeders, after all, have more time to devote to their animals. You may find that your pet shop has a list of keepers in your area, or you may be able to find a name and address in a pet magazine, or even in your local newspaper. Do not forget to contact your local pet welfare centre and the local zoo – you may find that they have animals that they would be happy for you to give a home to.

Bear in mind that chipmunks will be easier to obtain at certain times of the year than at other times. Young animals will only be available eight to twelve weeks after the start of the breeding season. As chipmunks breed, on average, twice a year in captivity, young stock will only be available in mid-to-late spring and in late summer to early autumn.

2 *A Home For Your Chipmunk*

As already mentioned, the chipmunk is one of the many species of ground squirrel and, in the wild, they generally live in the lower canopy of the forest, rarely venturing above six feet from the ground, and digging burrows in the roots of trees for storing food and for winter hibernation. During the warmer months of the year, they nest in trees, but in the winter they prefer burrows filled with leaf litter, dry grasses etc. With this in mind, there is little need to build cages any higher than six feet for your chipmunks, unless of course you intend to stand up in it yourself and, like me, are over six feet tall. They do well in smaller cages than this, and breed very well in cages 36 x 24 x 18 in, but that is not to say that this is the best-sized cage. I would always advise that you have as large a cage as possible in the space that you have available.

Chipmunks are best kept in pairs.

MIXING

I would recommend that you keep chipmunks in either single-sexed or opposite-sexed pairs. Colonies or groups of animals can be difficult, and require more knowledge than the beginner will

have. I have often found that a single animal will be picked on by other members of the group. This is not unusual and it would happen in the wild. However, in the wild, the persecuted individual could escape the attention of the others by moving away to a new part of the forest. In the artificial environment of the aviary, this is not possible, and the animal will suffer, and, in some cases, be killed by the other members of the colony. Should you find that one particular animal is being bullied more than others, then it may be a good idea to remove either the animal being bullied or the bully.

I have been asked whether different colours of chipmunks can be kept together. The answer to this is yes, but you should bear in mind that, on the whole, the dilute has a much more docile nature than the normal or cinnamon. However, this is not a hard and fast rule; as a friend of mine once remarked, animals cannot read what is being written about them, and so may break the 'rules'!

INDOOR CAGES

Quite elaborate cages can be made

A wire cage can be divided into different levels and partitions.

if you are any good at DIY. I have seen these made to fit into alcoves, across the corner of a room and along one end of a conservatory.

Remember that the chipmunk is a rodent, and rodents love to chew wood, particularly if bored. So, if you are making a cage yourself, take care to protect your walls. Suitable materials for your cage could be laminated blockboard to cover your walls, with a wire front and roof. The wire should be strong $1/2$ in square aviary wire. Do not use chicken wire as chipmunks are quite capable of chewing through this. A tray on the floor for a deep litter of wood shavings, which can be removed for cleaning without disturbing the residents too much, should be provided. The positioning of a sheet of glass or clear plastic part-way up the front of the cage will prevent spillage on to the floor outside the cage. Slides for the glass panel and doors should be constructed from 2 cm x 1 cm angle iron, screwed into place.

A wire partition can also be devised to separate the cage into two levels. This can then be inserted to confine the animals to the upper or lower half of the cage when cleaning out.

Alternatively, all-wire cages may be built using strong wire that is rigid enough to stand on its own. Recently, some very nice cages for chipmunks have begun to appear on the market and these are usually of the all-wire type. They are usually very suitable for the animals, provided that they are of adequate size – and not all are.

Naturally, all-wire cages are not too warm, and so you will need to put some thought into the position of the cage. Indoor cages can be placed in a number of different locations; for example, in an alcove in the living room, in a spare bedroom or study or in a well-ventilated conservatory. In general, the area should be draught-free and out of direct sunlight, and yet should be both well ventilated and have some sunlight, as chipmunks like to sunbathe if it is not too hot!

If your chipmunks are breeding, they may not take too well to much disturbance around the cage, and some females are not too keen on certain frequencies emitted by the television.

OUTDOOR CAGES

Outdoor cages or aviaries should, again, be as large as you can manage. Some authorities maintain that an outdoor cage

An outdoor aviary suitable for chipmunks.

should be no smaller than 6 feet square, but I have known chipmunks live and breed very well year after year in an outdoor cage of just 3 feet square. Naturally, in a large aviary you will be able to keep a colony rather than just a pair.

As with indoor cages, aviaries may be simple or complex, depending on the ability of the builder or what you are able to afford to buy. The basic structure is a rectangular aviary with a similar shed attached. Hardwood is best avoided as it can contain substances which are harmful to some rodents if chewed. In order to weatherproof the wood, use a polyurethane varnish – do not use phenol-based wood preservatives. Double entry doors are a useful additional safety precaution to prevent escapes. The wire used should be no larger than $^{1}/_{2}$ in x 1 in, although I must admit I prefer $^{1}/_{2}$ in x $^{1}/_{2}$ in.

The housing area of the outdoor cage should be made of sturdy wood, and can either be purpose-built or adapted from a garden shed. For extra warmth, it may be lined with hardboard or similar material. An external wired window allows extra ventilation, but must be able to be covered at night and in bad weather. Within the housing area, there should be

This large outdoor aviary makes an ideal home.

an indoor cage, which can be relatively small compared to that outside. Access to the outside from the housing area should be provided via a choice of routes, with one close to the ground and one at about shoulder height, and should be provided with ledges both inside and out.

The roof of the housing area is best covered in roofing felt, both for insulation and because other

Creating a natural habitat for your chipmunks will enhance their quality of life.

materials (such as corrugated metal) tend to be very noisy. A quarter to a half of the outside run should also be covered, this time with plastic sheeting, as should the entire northernmost side of the cage itself. This is to protect the animals from the worst of the wind and rain at all times of the year. However, outdoor enclosures must also have areas of shade that the chipmunks can retire to in the summer, and this is particularly so if the aviary is lined or roofed with plastic, as this will intensify the sun. The base of the cage may be wired and covered with a layer of soil, or can be concreted to prevent the animals from burrowing out, and to prevent vermin, such as rats, from burrowing in.

Artificial heating should not really be necessary for outside areas provided that adequate insulation and bedding materials are given when the temperature drops.

STORING FOOD

Like their larger cousins, the squirrels, chipmunks have an in-built desire and need to store food in preparation for both winter and leaner times. A good deep litter in which they can do this is vital for

A designated toilet area will help to keep the cage clean.

them. They may very well also choose a nest box for this. Failure to provide a storage area may cause the animal to carry food around in its pouches for long

Peat and hay provide good bedding material.

Branches should be located at different angles and heights to provide scope for climbing.

periods, and this could lead to damage to the lining of the pouches. The litter used on the base of the cage may be a mixture of wood shavings, moss peat and hay. Hay helps to prevent any tunnels that they may dig from collapsing. Do not use sawdust as this can cause quite bad eye infections. A depth of around 2-3 ins is ideal, and will allow plenty of digging and rooting about to take place.

To this, you can add a wide variety of different 'toys' in large outdoor areas – I would suggest an old tree stump, hollow logs, a small pile of logs, drainpipes and rocks. Above this, branches should be placed at various different angles and heights to provide the animals with plenty of climbing and gnawing areas. Branches should only be from safe trees, i.e. those of the various fruit trees. Do not remove the leaves, as the chipmunks will take great delight in doing that for themselves. Ensure that all items are firmly anchored and that no movement can occur that may cause a danger to your pets.

NEST BOXES

I supply several nest boxes in each cage – mone per animal and one spare, if space allows. These can be placed at various heights, but you will usually find that, in a colony, the most dominant animal will occupy the highest box. A few pieces of ceramic sewer pipe on

There should be a minimum of one nest box for each chipmunk.

and the slightly larger ones sold for lovebirds and similar-sized birds are used and enjoyed by my animals. The boxes can be part-filled, but I usually find that most animals are happier filling their own box, provided that enough nesting material is placed in the cage for them to use. This will be shredded and piled into the nest box.

Several different types of material can be used for chipmunks' bedding. Large wood shavings are the easiest, along with soft meadow hay; however, do not overlook other items. Things that my animals have used for bedding over the years are dried leaves of various plants, dried grass, soft paper tissue (ie. loo or kitchen roll) and shredded paper. Do not be tempted to provide them with either cotton wool or the cotton wool-type bedding. These, while they look warm, can be very dangerous to chipmunks if they are eaten or get caught around the foot or body of an animal.

the floor of the cage is also used for nesting, and chipmunks may also store food there. These pipes provide a very good retreat for young and lower-ranking animals in a colony. It is for this reason also that more than one entrance hole should be provided from the shed to the outside area.

Nest boxes can either be home-made or bought in a shop; however, it is unlikely that you will be able to purchase a nest box made especially for chipmunks. I find that those sold for small parrot-like birds are the best; both the small ones sold for budgies

CLEANING THE CAGE

Chipmunks are not difficult to keep clean and hygienic. By nature, they are fastidious little creatures and will usually use one

Remove the soiled litter.

elsewhere. If the enclosure is an outdoor one, the inclusion of peat in the litter will eliminate the odours of the decomposing urine.

There is no hard-and-fast rule as to when the cage of your animal should be cleaned. This usually depends on where the cage is sited, its size, number of inhabitants, and, last but not least, just how sensitive the noses of the owner and the rest of the family are. It really should not smell unpleasant, but if it does, you have left it too long! As a rough guide, a small indoor cage may well need a good clean out once a week, while a good-sized outdoor enclosure may only need to be

area of their cage as a loo. Often, this can be a spare, unused nest box or, in the case of one male I have, an empty food bowl. Provided that you clean this area regularly, they will not urinate

Newspaper can be used as a base.

A fresh supply of bedding will be needed.

Spread the litter to a depth of 2-3 inches.

Clean and tidy – ready for the chipmunks to use again.

cleaned once a month, although I would suggest that the loo be cleaned more often.

When cleaning, try not to remove too many of the food caches. Should you do this, it will make the chipmunks agitated and they may lose some confidence in you. Remember not to disturb the nest boxes in the breeding season. These should be left until after the babies are weaned, and then cleaned three or four more times in the year.

Cages should be washed with a mild disinfectant solution. There are a number of suitable types on the market that are designed for use with either birds or small mammals. Avoid those that are coal tar or phenol-based as these can be toxic to chipmunks. Cetavlon/cetrimide solutions are excellent for cleaning food dishes and water bottles. Always rinse and dry the food dishes before returning them to use.

3 *Getting To Know Your Chipmunk*

It is easy to sum up chipmunks by describing their behaviour. They are friendly, lively, agile creatures, possessing curiosity and a lack of caution, making them a very interesting animal to keep.

They are clever climbers with an almost infallible sense of balance – in my experience they rarely fall, although they are cautious of new things. After a visual inspection, the chipmunk will slowly and hesitantly approach an unfamiliar object, with the hind legs spread wide and the tail slowly waved horizontally over the body, ready for instant flight. This is not to say that they have a horror of strange things; indeed, they love something different to explore and play with, although they also enjoy a regular routine.

ROUTINE

Regular routine helps any chipmunk to become much more

Chipmunks are friendly by nature, and have an insatiable sense of curiosity.

at ease and friendly with you. They are diurnal in habit, emerging from their nest boxes at around dawn, and active for most of the day, with short rest periods on a branch, shelf or in the nest box before retiring by sunset. Even chipmunks kept in the house rarely emerge at night. Animals that are kept in outside aviaries will also spend more time in their nest boxes in bad weather, just as they do in the wild.

HANDLING

Generally, chipmunks resent being restrained and can give a nasty bite in protest if you suddenly grab. However, if you obtain your animals while they are still young (if possible, under 16 weeks of age), they will soon become hand-tamed and trusting, taking tidbits from your hand, and eventually becoming confident enough to sit on your open hand and eat, rather than rushing away with it. Provided that this confidence is not destroyed by your making a quick grab, certain animals will become very cheeky, sitting on your shoulders, exploring pockets and even attempting to hide peanuts in your ears.

The correct way to hold a chipmunk.

RESTRAINING

Should you have to restrain your chipmunk for any reason, such as for treatment or examination, then it is advisable to wear protective gloves. They do not have to be thick leather gauntlets; thick gardening gloves are just as good. If the glove is too thick you are likely to hold the animal too tight and this can lead to injury.

When catching an animal in a small cage, it is often easier just to use a soft cloth to trap and restrain it with the correct grip with bare hands. However, animals that are in larger cages or aviaries should be caught in a fine mesh net. Once captured, the more easily handled animals can be held in the hand with the second and third fingers over the shoulders, the joints of the fingers controlling the head movements. Alternatively, the thumb can be placed under the chin, gently pushing the jaws upwards, and thus preventing the animal from nipping. If this method is used, do not squeeze the throat. Do not restrain a chipmunk by the tail unless it is grasped at the very root. Any attempt to grip the animal along the length of the tail may result in the loose skin being torn off as the animal struggles. This is part of the species' natural defence against predators who have not been able

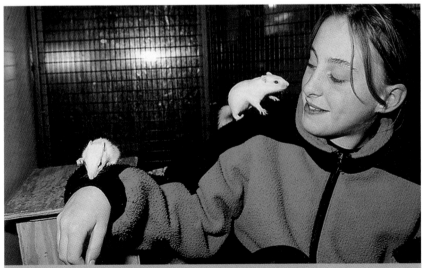

The more chipmunks are handled, the tamer they will become.

to get hold of the body of the animal. Should it happen by accident, the tail will heal very quickly of its own accord; the area left bare will gradually wither and drop off, leaving a clean stump.

For safety's sake, always restrain the animal over a surface such as a table, or in a seated position over your lap; then, if the animal does manage to get free, the drop will not be so far that it may injure itself.

TAMING

By far the easiest way to tame a chipmunk is via its stomach — they are almost obsessed with food! If you have a large cage that will allow you to actually get in with your chipmunks, then so much the better. Enter the cage bearing tidbits such as raisins, nuts, etc. Take a seat and place some of the tidbits around your feet. The animals will come and take the food and then gradually, if you offer the treats from your hand, they will begin to hold on to a finger while they accept the food. Gradually, their fear will become less and less, and they will begin to climb on your feet and lap, eventually climbing all over you looking for more food. Avoid sudden movements which may

No self-respecting chipmunk can resist a tasty treat.

startle them. Once they are used to you and associate you with the tidbits, then it will be difficult for you to get into the cage without having them climbing all over you.

If your pets are kept in a smaller cage, training can be more difficult, but not impossible. It will often entail sitting or standing for long periods with your hand through the cage door. First, place some of the tidbits a little distance from your fingers and then gradually progress until you are holding them and have them in the palm of your hand. You may get the occasional nip – if so, try not to yell too loudly!

Generally, chipmunks do not bite for no reason. If held too tightly they may become frightened and nip your finger. Their teeth are so sharp that this can be extremely painful. Most chipmunks will look at you a couple of seconds after nipping you as if to ask what all the fuss is about. They are not nasty animals and do not bite for the sake of it. A word of warning: people do seem to feel compelled to poke their fingers through the bars of the cage to tickle and coo at the chipmunks. Your chipmunk is likely to assume that a piece of food is being offered to it, and bite. Should this happen to you or to a member of your family, do not get upset, the finger should not have been in the cage in the first place!

OUT OF THE CAGE

The Siberian chipmunk makes a wonderful and very entertaining pet, but it is not a cuddly lap pet, and you cannot teach it tricks or take it for walks – do not buy a chipmunk if you have this sort of thing in mind. They cannot be given free run of your house for any length of time, although some tame animals can be allowed out of their cage for short periods. I am often asked how this can be achieved. It is difficult, and it takes much time and effort. Firstly, your chipmunk must be very tame. As already mentioned, chipmunks are very greedy animals, especially where nuts are concerned. Start by holding a peanut or hazelnut through the wire of the cage. Be patient, as this can take a while. If the chipmunk does not come, drop the nut into the cage. Over time, the animal will get to realise that the nut is coming from your hand and will take it directly from your fingers. Do not spend too much time each day on this, or

Careful preparations must be made if your chipmunk is to be allowed outside his cage.

your animal will have too many nuts. Throughout this stage of the training, talk to your chipmunk, as this will attract its attention. Once you are sure that your pet is coming to you without fear, then you can move on.

Before you can release your chipmunk, you must take a careful look at your chosen room. It must be sealed, including the chimney. Remember that even a gas fire has a chimney of some kind. Ornaments that can be knocked over should be removed, as should house plants. Although the chipmunk will not eat them, they will consider them a fine place to hide their peanuts, and this can make a very nice mess.

On the day, do not feed your pet and begin operations fairly late in the afternoon. Open the cage door and feed a single nut to your

Returning the chipmunk to his cage can take some coaxing.

chipmunk through the entrance. Move away, leaving the door ajar. The chipmunk will not usually rush out; it will be a slow and nervous affair, with several false starts. Do not force it out; let your pet emerge in its own good time, with no interference. It must feel safe, so please do be patient.

At first, everything is new and potentially dangerous to your pet. It will show its agitated state by fluffing out its tail like a bottle-brush, and waving it back and

Chipmunks get most of their exercise playing with each other.

forth across its back. It will soon regain its confidence, and start investigating every nook and cranny. Once it has settled, offer it a nut from your hand. If it will not come to you, do not force the issue, but place the nut on the floor until your chipmunk has

The curious chipmunk will investigate all new things in his cage.

found it. Be careful not to provide too much food, or your chipmunk will not want to go back to its cage until all the food has been hidden.

Returning the chipmunk to its cage can, at first, take much coaxing, and may well involve catching the little devil. The best way to avoid this is to have your cage at ground level or to provide a ramp of some form to the cage door, and it is helpful if your pet is used to the rattle of its food dish being filled. Once the animal is back in its cage, resist the urge to rush to the door to shut it. If you frighten the chipmunk at this point, you may not succeed in teaching it to return to the cage when you want it to. If it comes out again before you can shut the door, wait a while and try again. It will return, especially when it gets hungry or thirsty.

Eventually, your chipmunk's

Pine cones may be appreciated

natural greed and curiosity will bring it into physical contact with you. That is, it will eventually jump on you. They move very fast, and you may very well find that your pet suddenly appears on your lap and, just as quickly, is gone again. At first, it will not stay too long, but, with a little patience and a few nuts, it will eventually stay for longer. Once you reach this stage, your chipmunk will probably allow you to handle it a little. This, in turn, makes returning it to the cage that much easier.

A hay-net makes an interesting addition to the cage.

Some chipmunks enjoy working out on exercise wheels.

Although tame chipmunks will tolerate a limited amount of petting and stroking, they are usually far too active to sit still for more than a few seconds. The value of the chipmunk as a pet comes from their active and lively way of life.

TOYS

I am often asked about suitable toys for Siberian chipmunks. Most small animals, such as the Syrian hamster, are easy to buy toys for. However, it is more difficult to make suggestions for chipmunks, not because they do not play, but because their play tends to consist of tag and chase games. Some chipmunks will play with some items, where others will completely ignore them.

Natural toys, such as pine cones, are always a good idea, and these

can be dangled from the roof of the cage or placed on the floor. Hopefully, they will be chewed and thrown around.

Some chipmunks, particularly those in indoor cages, will use exercise wheels. The wheel will need to be large in order to avoid injuring the chipmunk's tail, and it should be hung on the side of the cage or aviary rather than being placed on the floor.

Items suspended from the roof of the cage, which the animals can run through and hide in, are generally popular. This would include hollow pipes and thick rope, which can also be piled on the floor of the cage. I have seen chipmunks play with empty coconut shells, and use hanging baskets as sunbathing sites in an outdoor aviary. If you are looking for toys for your chipmunk, the answer is to try what you have in mind, provided that it is safe, as your chipmunks may like it.

Feeding Your Chipmunk

In the wild, the diet of the chipmunk varies greatly, depending on the areas in which they are found and the time of year. It would, however, include seeds, nuts, various different types of vegetation, the bark from some trees, shoots, berries, various insects, grubs, worms, some small birds, their eggs and chicks and even some small mammals. With all this in mind, it is not difficult to realise that it is very important that you offer your chipmunks a varied and healthy diet, as they cannot go off and find it for themselves.

Chipmunks need a varied and healthy diet.

THE ESSENTIALS

So what constitutes a good diet for a chipmunk, bearing in mind all the different things that they are known to feed on in the wild? This chapter gives details of the essentials that you must provide to keep your chipmunks happy and healthy.

EQUIPMENT

The food should be provided in pottery bowls that cannot be easily overturned. In outdoor aviaries they should be positioned so that

A ceramic food bowl is the best choice.

A supply of fresh water can be supplied with a water bottle.

the food is protected from the weather. I would also suggest that a bowl be provided in both the indoor and the outdoor areas. Water should be available at all times, in water bottles with metal spouts, and again I would suggest that a bottle be placed in each area of the cage.

CARBOHYDRATES

As chipmunks are very active, they burn up a great deal of energy as they leap about from place to place. Carbohydrates are a good source of energy and approximately 50 per cent of their food intake should be made up of carbohydrate-rich foods. For example, include cereals such as maize, oats, wheat and corn, and also some forms of dog biscuit (which also help keep the teeth worn down), and some of the

Oats.

seeds sold for small birds. Of course, as with humans, an excessive intake of these carbohydrates beyond the daily need will lead to the animals becoming fat. While they require a certain amount of fat to help protect them from the cold of the winter, too much weight will shorten their lives and may also prevent them from breeding.

On the other hand, too little

Flaked maize.

Mixed biscuits.

Bread and crispbread.

carbohydrate intake will cause the animal to obtain its energy supply by the breakdown of fats in the body, which can also be dangerous.

The other 50 per cent of the chipmunk's diet should consist of fats, protein, vitamins and minerals.

FATS

Fats are required in the diet to provide essential fatty acids, to act as a carrier for the fat-soluble vitamins, and also to provide protection from cold, as mentioned above.

Sources of fat for chipmunks are the oil-rich nuts – peanuts, hazelnuts, almonds and walnuts. Acorns are also a good source of fat, but I have found that many of

Walnuts provide a source of fat.

A dried food mix can be obtained for chipmunks.

PROTEIN

Protein is what the muscles of the body are made of. In active animals, the muscles are in constant use and thus in a constant state of wear and tear. Proteins are also required to form certain enzymes and hormones. Protein can be obtained from both the plant and animal sources in their diet.

The best forms of protein come in the form of insects, and I find that my own chipmunks love mealworms. In fact, I have tamed more animals via the treat of a mealworm (or two or three!) a night than by any other method. At one time, it was very difficult

my chipmunks are not too keen on these as they can be rather bitter. Sunflower seeds are also high in oils and are certainly a firm favourite of the chipmunks, but they should not be fed in too large an amount as they also have very low levels of calcium. Corn is also very high in fat and chipmunks seem to be very fond of fresh corn on the cob. Raw egg may be given once a week, but some animals appear to like this more than others.

Insufficient fats in the diet will result in slow reproduction, poor, dry skin, often with flaky patches, and a dull coat.

Corn cobs are a great favourite.

Fresh fruit and vegetables supply protein to the diet.

Garden flowers can provide an interesting addition.

A multi-vitamin supplement.

These should, however, only be fed in small amounts.

VITAMINS AND MINERALS

The majority of the vitamins and minerals required by your chipmunks are found in most foods. However, I also supply my animals with vitamin and mineral additives. These can be obtained from most pet shops, either in the form of powder that you can sprinkle on the food, or as drops that can be added to the water.

VARIETY

Below is a list of the items of food that my own chipmunks have eaten at some point, so try these on yours and see what they like and dislike. However, remember, like children with sweets, chipmunks will, if allowed, only eat the things they particularly like and disregard the rest. Vary their diet so that they do not get bored.

Sunflower seeds, wheat, oats, maize, rye, canary seeds, buckwheat, melon seeds, peanuts, hazelnuts, walnuts, cobnuts, beechmast, acorns, pine nuts, almonds, brazil nuts, pecans, oranges, apples, pears, cherries, grapes, gooseberries, blackberries, raspberries, strawberries, red, black and white currants, peaches,

to obtain good supplies of healthy mealworms, but now most good pet shops will stock, or be able to obtain, disease-free mealworms that you can feed to your pets. Some chipmunks will also take small crickets and locusts, but some chipmunks are keener on these than others, and should they miss one or two you may find crickets or locusts crawling about the house. Of course this is no problem if your chipmunks are housed outside.

Proteins are also found in nuts, cereals, fruits and vegetables. Other items that can be fed and that are a good source of protein are dried cat and dog foods and cooked chicken or lean mince.

dried banana, sultanas, raisins, apricots and plums (do not feed the stones of plums as they contain cyanide and can be dangerous), tomatoes, peas, beans, corn on the cob, lettuce, bean sprouts, dandelions, chickweed, rose hips and haws, nasturtium flowers, rose petals, and the list goes on!

RECIPE

Should you wish to make a mixture of your own for your animals, here is a suggested recipe.

5 lb good quality hamster or gerbil mixture
$1^{1}/_{2}$ lb sunflower seeds
$1^{1}/_{2}$ lb peanuts, shelled and unshelled
1 lb maize
2 lb canary seed and millet
1 lb tropical dried fruit mix
$^{1}/_{2}$ lb mixed nuts.

5 Breeding Chipmunks

If you intend to breed chipmunks, you will have to take several factors into account. Your first consideration is the space that you have available. Is the cage (or cages) large enough for a whole family of animals, or do you intend to sell the offspring and, if so, how easy or difficult will this be?

Careful consideration must be given to selecting breeding stock.

THE PAIR

Should you decide that you do have the space to breed, then it is important that you have the correct animals for breeding. Just to breed from two animals that happen to be male and female can lead to all sorts of problems. Therefore, the actual decision to breed or not to breed should ideally be made before you have acquired any stock.

If at all possible, you should begin by obtaining two animals that are not related. Check where you are buying the animals from and ask if they are able to supply unrelated pairs. If not, then it may be wise for you to purchase a single animal and go elsewhere for the mate. Of course, it is more difficult to obtain this type of information from a pet shop than from a private breeder, but the latter are not always that easy to find. If you are lucky enough to find a breeder, you should be able to view not only the young stock available but also the parents. This will give you an opportunity to observe the parents' temperaments and spot any problems that may be present.

GENETICS

Breeding chipmunks is not difficult, but obtaining the correct stock and the correct data on breeding can be. While I do not wish to confuse you, it is important, if you are going to breed, that you understand a little about genetics. This is particularly important if you do decide that you are going to breed for one or other of the colour mutations. The wild colour of any animal is always known as 'Agouti', and this is the name of the 'normal' coloured chipmunk. The normal colour is sandy-brown, with paler, greyish belly fur. It has five very prominent brown-black stripes running from the shoulder to the rump, and stripes running from the nose, around the eyes, to the base of the ear. However, nature occasionally creates variations in the form of mutations (new colours), and this has happened with the Siberian chipmunk. Although at the present time there are only two mutations available, it is highly likely that, as they become more widely retained, more colour and possibly coat mutations will occur. Often these different mutations can be combined to create even more. However, so far this has not occurred with the chipmunk. The two new colours currently available in the UK are the Dilute White and the Cinnamon.

DILUTE WHITE: Often incorrectly called Albino. It is not an Albino as it has light, biscuit-coloured stripes on the face and back, and a similar-coloured tail. The eyes are a ruby-red rather than the bright pink of an Albino. Genetically, this colour mutation is recessive, a term I shall explain in a moment.

CINNAMON: There are various different views of this colour; some people believe that it is a true mutation, while others believe that it is a throwback to a sub-species of animal that was obtained from the island of Hokkaido in Japan. Basically, it is an animal where a lot of the black in the coat has been changed to a rusty brown and the brown in the normal coat has been turned to orange. The eyes are dark and this colour is also recessive.

There are two forms of inheritance in breeding animals – recessive and dominant, the recessive being the most common form. A colour is known to be recessive when it disappears in crosses with the original wild colour 'Agouti'. In the Siberian chipmunk, this occurs with both the Dilute White and the

Dilute White Siberian chipmunk.

A normal chipmunk (left) and a Cinnamon.

Cinnamon. Let me explain. When a Dilute White is mated to an Agouti, the youngsters which result are all Agouti, like the Agouti parent. This proves that, in combination with each other, the Agouti is dominant and the Dilute is recessive. If mated together, the youngsters will give birth to 75 per cent Agouti young and 25 per cent Dilute. However, if you mate the same youngsters back to the Dilute parent, they will give birth to 50 per cent Agouti and 50 per cent Dilute young.

So, with recessive inheritance, a colour is not necessarily lost if it does not appear in the young. An Agouti born from Agouti and

Dilute (or Cinnamon) parents can be 'split'. This means that it carries the gene for another colour. For example, if you mate an Agouti to a Dilute, the young should be Agouti, as this is dominant, as explained above. If the litter includes three Agouti and one Dilute, then you know that the Agouti is 'split' or a 'carrier' of Dilute.

This shows what is known as the typical 3:1 ratio, which plays an important part in genetics. The fact that the Dilute does not reappear until the second generation need not worry the breeder because once it has recurred, the Dilute youngsters are true-breeding and will not revert to the Agouti if mated together.

SEXING

Chipmunks are not too difficult to sex if you know what you are looking for. One of the first things that you have to do is to persuade your animals to turn upside down so that those vital areas are on view. They should do this quite happily as part of their normal behaviour, but the problem is to get them to stay in that position long enough for you to have a good look. It is probably best done when they are clinging to the wire of the cage. A great deal depends on your judgement of the distance between the anus and the urethra, the vagina in the female and the penis in the male.

In the female, the distance is only about 5 mm, while in the male it is about 20 mm. It is comparatively easy if you have one animal of each sex to compare, but quite often this is not the case and I have known more than one person getting very confused trying to tell the sexes apart when, in fact, they actually had babies of only one sex. Of course the chipmunks were not in the least bit confused.

Once the breeding season commences, the testes of the mature males descend into the scrotum and then they are very much more obvious. In adult females that have had a litter, the mammary glands may be more obvious for the rest of that year. So look carefully when buying stock – if you want a young animal, look for one that obviously has not been bred from.

Chipmunks in the nest can be sexed almost from the time of birth, but do not attempt this until they are at least ten days of age, and then only when mother is out of the nest, unless she is very used to you and very tame. Handle the babies very carefully. I usually rub my hands in the nesting material to get more of the chipmunks' smell on my hands than my smell on to the babies. While they are small and hairless, not only are they easy to sex but they do not bite. Just turn them over and you will easily be able to tell the boys from the girls.

WHEN TO BREED

Chipmunks reach maturity and are ready for breeding in the year following their birth. So, maturity is reached at between six and twelve months of age, depending on the time of year that they were

A female chipmunk.

A male chipmunk.

born. For example, those born in the spring of one year will usually breed in the spring of the following year, while those born in the autumn will also usually breed the following spring. The beginning of the cycle is seasonally influenced. As the days grow longer and the nights grow shorter, and as the air temperature rises, hormonal changes will take place in the animals.

You can expect breeding activity among animals retained outside to commence shortly after the end of their winter torpidity. Most matings occur in March and April for litters in May and June, and again in July and August for litters in September and October. Animals housed indoors will not have had a true hibernation period and so will usually begin to breed that much earlier. Some pairs or groups in this situation will often breed all year and produce three litters a year. However, I would not advise that this situation is encouraged as it can lead to over-breeding of the female, possibly causing her early death. She must be given enough time to regain her condition between litters.

MATING
Once spring arrives, the females

will begin to come into season, and will make no attempt to hide the fact. The female chipmunk in season will tell all, by chirping loudly from the highest point in the cage, although the males near to her will be aware of the situation well before you are. About twenty-four hours before she actually starts to call, she will be of interest to the males, but she is unlikely to allow them to get close or familiar. The next day, however, she will be ready for mating and she will make her condition very plain by calling any available male with her high chirp.

At first, you may wonder what on earth this noise is and be looking around the garden for some strange bird, but, once heard, the call is not easily forgotten. She will repeat the series of chirps throughout the day, and will mate with any male that can catch her. In an outdoor enclosure with more than a single male, this can lead to fighting among them. She may mate several times at five to ten-minute intervals with one male and then, when he has lost interest, she will mate with another. So if you wish to breed from a particular pair they must be caged on their own. The female will continue to chirp even after several matings and, if the male refuses and sits quietly grooming or feeding, then she will approach him very blatantly and flaunt herself in front of him. She will strut around stiff-legged, with her tail fluffed out and lashing in a slightly annoyed manner, until he regains interest, at which point she is likely to dash off shouting over her shoulder that now he will have to catch her.

The following day, she will still be of interest to the males but will have regained her aloof exterior and refuse to have anything to do with them. Use a calendar to keep track of the breeding of your animals. The first matings of the season often prove unsuccessful, usually because the males are not yet in prime condition, but the second matings are usually successful.

PREGNANCY

Within the first ten days of pregnancy, the female will begin to show a slight enlargement of the lower mammary glands. After about twenty to twenty-five days, the glands further up the abdomen will also become more noticeable and, at this point, there may be some widening around the girth of the animal. During the final

The female chipmunk will chirp loudly to advertise that she is in season.

week of the pregnancy, the belly will become a little more stretched and the fur may appear a little thin. Gestation usually lasts from 28 to 35 days.

Throughout her pregnancy, the female will build up her nest box ready for the big day. You must, therefore, ensure that she is provided with lots of safe, warm nesting material and also a little extra food for her to hide away. This extra food will be stored in the nest box and will be used by the female to feed on for the first day or two after the birth, as she will rarely leave the babies for the first 36-48 hours.

THE BIRTH

The female will usually give birth quite happily away from prying eyes and you must be content to let her get on with it. Just listen, do not look. You will undoubtedly hear her scrabbling around in the box, trying to get herself into the most comfortable position. In the period just before birth, she may decide that the nest is not quite

During her pregnancy, the female will build up nesting material in the nest box.

right and needs more bedding, so ensure that more is available.

Be patient and eventually you will hear the squeaks of the newborn. Do not disturb the nest, as the mother will tidy up and eat the placenta. Do not attempt to see how many babies she has had at this stage, as this may well lead to her abandoning the nest and the babies or, worse still, eating the litter, no matter how tame and trusting she normally is of you. The female will emerge from the box just as soon as she is ready, usually when she is hungry or thirsty and happy that the babies are warm, content and safe. Even at this point, do not look; she may only be out of the way for a minute or so and, if she finds signs of disturbance when she returns, she may either destroy her young or move them elsewhere away from what she regards as the predator – you!

AFTER THE BIRTH

Should your chipmunks be housed in even a reasonably-sized cage, then it is usually fine to leave the male in the cage with the female. Of course, if the animals are in a large aviary then the problem does not arise, as the male will be able to make himself scarce and keep away from the female. If you have a very dominant female, it is sometimes best to remove the male, although, as yet, I have not had to do this. The female may become aggressive towards the male in an attempt to keep him away from the young, and she will certainly dominate the food and bedding. I usually find that, although the female will not allow the male access to the babies when they are very young, once they are a week or so old she will allow him into the nest box and, very often, leave him keeping the babies warm while she ventures out to stretch her legs and get some food. One Dilute White male of mine has been present in the nest box with the mother and babies from day one, and has been known to help the female move them from the nest box in the outside enclosure to the warmer situation of the nest box in the shed.

LOOKING AT THE BABIES

Once the female has been in and

Babies are born blind and hairless.

out of the nest a few times and begins to return to normal feeding and hoarding in other areas of the cage, you can take a quick peek at the young. Be warned – at first it must be quick, as she will not venture far and usually will have one eye on the nest box and probably the other on you. If she sees anything suspicious, she will come running back to the nest to investigate what is going on. If she finds things not to her liking, she may well move or destroy the litter to keep them, to her mind, safe; so take care.

The litter will be well buried under the bedding material in order to keep them warm. Carefully pull this back in such a way that you can replace it later. As soon as they are uncovered, they will start to squeak and protest and will move around in an attempt to get back under cover. Should the female hear them piping, then she will return. She will at first check the entrance hole to see if anyone has used it. Of course you have not, as the nest box will have either a removable lid or wall to enable you to look in. If you can cover up the young and close the box before she gets back, she may very well have quite a sniff and look

around and adjust the covering over the young, and then return to what she was doing. Once you have managed this a few times, she will begin to get used to you doing it and probably take very little notice, provided that you leave everything as she expects to find it. However, I would suggest that you do not look at the babies more than once a day.

DEVELOPMENT

Newborn babies are hairless and blind. Those that are going to be normally marked will have dark backs and pink stomachs, while the Dilute will be pink all over. At this stage, Cinnamon babies are indistinguishable from the normally marked.

By the time they are a week old, they will be gaining a fine downy coat which is fully through in about 14 to 18 days. At this point, the babies' eyes will still be closed and they will blunder around the nest when it is tampered with. At 16 days, the babies look like miniature adults, but their eyes are still closed. They will eventually open at 26 to 28 days, quite late in their development. From about the age of five weeks, the babies will begin to leave the nest box. At this point I usually ensure that there is plenty of climbing material just outside the nest box entrance to give them something to rest on and thus prevent a fall. It is during the next few days that they will learn from their mother how to forage for their own food and learn where to find water. Of course, up until they have left the nest, the mother (and occasionally the father) will have been bringing food to the nest for the youngsters. They may still suckle from their mother for a few days but, as they grow, the mother's milk will dry up and they are forced to take more and more solid foods.

By the time they are six weeks of age, the young chipmunks will be totally independent of the mother – but do not be tempted to remove the babies too soon; the mother will still be showing them what to eat and how to nest-build etc. for a couple more weeks, and I would recommend that they are not removed until the age of eight to ten weeks.

A SECOND LITTER

Many females will produce a second litter in a year, particularly if it is a good summer with plenty of warm weather and lots of good food. The litter will usually be born around August as, by this time, the mother will have been able to gain weight and condition with the good summer feeding.

A female may produce a second litter.

These second litters are often smaller in numbers than the first. They will develop in the same time span as the earlier litters, but, as they are born later, they will not be ready to leave the nest until the middle of October and can suffer if there is an early cold spell in the autumn. It is very important, therefore, that the animals are getting plenty of food and that the nest box has a good supply of bedding.

If you want to avoid having a second litter, you will need to separate the breeding pair before the birth of the first litter, which can cause problems with the raising of the litter. I would therefore advise that you prepare yourself for two litters, or that you do not breed at all.

HAND-REARING

For a number of different reasons, you may find that it is necessary to think about hand-rearing a baby. Unfortunately there is very little that has been written on the hand-rearing of squirrels, let alone chipmunks, but it is possible to hand-rear a Siberian chipmunk. It is difficult and can be very tiring, and often, sadly, the babies will not survive, but it is always worth a try.

The most important thing to remember if you are to be successful is that the babies will require feeding regularly. Animals as small as newborn chipmunks only require tiny amounts of food, and because of this, they need feeding very frequently. If you are considering hand-rearing, you must realise that it can be a time-consuming business. Remember that until the babies are three weeks of age, they will require feeding every three hours, day and night. At four weeks, the early or the middle night feed can be abandoned, but should the baby be the smallest, the runt of the litter, you may need to increase the number of feeds from every three hours to every two.

To feed, you will need to use a dropper. These can be obtained from the pet store and will be those marketed for small kittens, and you will require the smallest that you can obtain. When actually feeding the baby, you must do so very slowly and watch very carefully all the time for bubbles at the nostrils or the sounds of choking, as this will indicate that the food is not entering the stomach but the lungs instead. Should this happen, do not panic; hold the baby gently by

When they leave the nest, the young are very nervous.

the hind legs until the lungs are clear. Do not overfeed – little and often is best. It is difficult to give exact amounts, but the baby's stomach should appear full, though not bloated.

After every feed, lightly stroke the baby's stomach. Stroke towards the tail with a damp, warm piece of cotton wool to stimulate the bowels.

Between feedings the babies should be kept in a box, in a nest made of soft tissue, and lightly covered so as to allow air to get to them. The box must be kept in a warm, but not hot, place.

WHAT TO FEED

When hand-rearing, it is important to maintain nourishment. It is also important, however, that you avoid feeding food that is too rich as this will cause stomach problems and can lead to the death of the young. At present, there is no special food preparation for the hand-rearing of rodents, and so it is up to you and trial and error, and the following suggestions.

Day 1-7: 1 part of evaporated milk to 2 parts water, with a pinch of glucose powder.

Day 8-30: 4 teaspoons of baby cereal; 1 teaspoon evaporated milk; $^1/_2$ teaspoon honey or glucose powder. This should be mixed together to the consistency of a gruel. Alternatively, a prepared milk rearing food made for kittens may be used.

6 *Health Care*

Chipmunks, if kept clean and supplied with a healthy, well-balanced diet and good, draught-free conditions with plenty of bedding when required, are normally healthy and very hardy little individuals. However, as with all animals, illness does occur and this can be caused by many different things. The most common causes are poor living conditions, diet and stress. Bad hygiene – not cleaning out regularly, or allowing food to rot – will attract insects to the cage, and these will undoubtedly be carrying disease. In turn, these will contaminate foods and lead to

infections of the digestive system.

Unfortunately, keeping chipmunks in outdoor aviaries will attract wild rodents and birds, and their droppings can cause such bacterial infections as salmonella and Tyzers disease. Therefore, the wire must be small enough not only to prevent your chipmunks from escaping, but also to prevent access to animals like mice and other creatures smaller than the chipmunks.

The following is a short list of ailments that your chipmunks may encounter. Remember, should your chipmunk appear ill and if you are unsure what to do, please do not have a wild guess and try to treat it yourself. Take it straight away to your local veterinary surgeon. Most of the illnesses mentioned can be prevented, and prevention is better than cure.

WOUNDS AND CUTS

As with most small mammals, a chipmunk's flesh heals very quickly and slight cuts and wounds are not in themselves dangerous at all.

The most common causes of these wounds tend to be the sharp edges of climbing and bedding materials, the cage edges and slight fights. Serious wounds can occur when chipmunks who do not know each other are introduced, and at these times great care must be taken. Only very deep wounds will need to be dealt with by a vet, as the stress of catching and taking the animal to the vet for a small wound is often more dangerous than the wound itself. Most cuts can be bathed in a mild antiseptic solution once a day. This may, of course, warrant removing the individual animal from a large cage or aviary to a small 'hospital' cage, unless your animals are very tame and used to being handled. If they are not and the wound is a slight one, just keep a close eye on it to make sure that there is no infection, and allow nature to heal the wound on its own.

DIARRHOEA

Diarrhoea can be caused by a number of different situations; in the worst cases, the animal may have caught an infection and will dehydrate rapidly which, in turn, can cause death. Should your chipmunk have both diarrhoea and small amounts of blood in the droppings, then it must be taken to the vet at once.

However, occasional loose droppings will occur from over-indulgence in citrus fruits or green vegetables. This can easily be remedied by withholding the fruit and vegetables and adding arrowroot or cornflour to the dried food. Raspberry leaves also act as an aid in settling stomachs and are highly regarded by some chipmunks.

CONSTIPATION

Constipation can be caused by too much dried food in the diet. It can be a major problem at weaning, and young animals may well

become slightly dehydrated. Ensure that your chipmunks are able to find the water bottle and to use it. In addition, add small amounts of apple, grapes or orange to the diet and this should prevent and remedy the situation before it occurs. Cod liver oil on the food can help in some cases.

Constipation can also be caused by the unsuitability of some forms of bedding, such as cotton wool, wood waste, kapok, etc. All bedding should be replaced with good, soft meadow hay, and fresh foods should be given in larger amounts than usual. Should the abdomen become swollen and the condition not change within 24 hours, then consult your vet.

SKIN PROBLEMS

Fleas and lice are not usually found on chipmunks, but there is a possibility that they may be picked up from wild rats or mice, or even the house cat, should any of these visit the cage.

Skin infections such as mange can be contracted from wild visitors as well as from infected pets. Mange is caused by a microscopic mite, which buries itself into the skin, causing intense irritation and sore areas. The usual cause of this is infected bedding.

Ringworm is a fungal infection and may also arrive on bedding. The infection causes hair loss in patches, with dry, flaky areas at the edges and inflammation from the scratching. Should either mange or ringworm be suspected, then your should consult your vet.

Generally, most chipmunk skin problems are caused by an imbalanced diet, and you should seek your vet's advice.

CHEEK POUCH PROBLEMS

The lining of the cheek pouches is very delicate and easily damaged. If this happens, it is usually caused by sharp objects being placed in the pouch; as these will scratch the lining and cause an infection. Abscesses in the pouches will cause a swelling which, at first, may well be mistaken for hoarded food. The area will feel hard and yet warm to the touch and the surface of the skin will appear reddish. Discharges from the abscess may be swallowed and this can cause more problems. The area should be lanced, by the vet, from the outside as soon as it is diagnosed. Once opened, this will be left to drain and the area will need to be bathed and dressed with antibiotics two or three times a day.

OVERGROWN TEETH

On rare occasions, chipmunks' teeth may become overgrown due to the overfeeding of soft foods. Should this happen, the chipmunk should be taken to the vet for the teeth to be trimmed. The animal's diet should be changed to include a much higher proportion of hard nuts and biscuits, on which the teeth will be worn down.

Even rarer are misaligned teeth. This condition is usually caused when the teeth or jaw have been damaged in an accident or fight. In many of these cases, the clipping of the teeth will have to be performed at least once a month, and this can cause a great deal of stress to the chipmunk. Should this be the case, it may be kinder to ask your vet to put it to sleep.

HEATSTROKE

Rodents can suffer from heatstroke surprisingly rapidly. An animal with heatstroke will appear uncoordinated in its movement and will seem generally unwell, and will soon die of heart failure if not quickly cooled down. In order to do this, place the animal in cool water until it shows signs of reviving. Dry the coat and place the animal in a cool, draught-free room until normal activity returns. Animals in outdoor enclosures must have areas of shade that they can retire to, and this is particularly so if the aviary is lined or roofed with plastic, as this will intensify the sun. Ensure that indoor cages are not standing in direct sunlight.

Dilute chipmunks can suffer sunburn if they sunbathe too much, particularly on the nose and the ears, so these strains need extra shade.

CARE DURING HIBERNATION

In the autumn, when the temperatures begin to fall, chipmunks begin to prepare for hibernation. There is a marked increase in hoarding activities, and they will begin to gain weight. Animals that are kept in outdoor enclosures all year, without access to a heated accommodation area, will often hibernate, if only for a few days. This is usually in their nest box or, if they have a deep peat or soil-based cage, they may burrow into this, much as they would in the wild. Providing the animals are of a good weight, have a good supply of bedding and winter foods and a frost-free area in which they can nest, hibernation will not harm them.

However, if you have only recently acquired your animal, I would not allow it to hibernate just in case it has not gained enough weight. To prevent it from hibernating, move the chipmunk to a heated shed with no access to the outside, or to a warm area of the house. You may still find that your animal hibernates for a single day at a time, which should present no problem. In fact, chipmunks do not hibernate all

winter, but rather for odd days when the weather is particularly bad.

OLDER ANIMALS

As with every other living thing, the possibility of unexpected illnesses increases with the chipmunk's age. However, the older chipmunk must receive just as much care and attention as the younger ones.

While writing this book, something happened to one of my oldest male chipmunks that I have never encountered before, nor found any reference to. This particular male is very tame, having been handled by necessity from quite a young age – his mother, in an over-indulgent mood, chewed off his ear flaps, and so he needed applications of antibiotic creams. He has been a very good stud male and has sired a great many of my animals. This summer is his seventh and, a short while ago, I went to check on the animals, as I do every morning, and found that he had suffered a stroke during the night. This was later confirmed by the vet. He is still very healthy and eats well, but he is now living in retirement on his own as the stroke has left him with his head cocked to one side. He is now unable to compete with his cage-mates for food, and needs the branches in the cage to be closer together as he finds the distance difficult to judge. So, should an old chipmunk of yours have a stroke, do not give up on them.

Generally, older animals will require more warmth, and possibly more areas on which to climb as their jumping abilities may be limited. I usually move animals over four years old into smaller cages and move them either into the house or into a heated shed, rather than allowing them to remain outside during the winter or bad weather. Most chipmunks die rather suddenly, usually during the winter, when things get too much for them. It is very sad to lose what you will have come to think of as very good friend, but please do not let me put you off. The Siberian chipmunk is a wonderful pet, and I hope that you have as much enjoyment keeping yours as I have had keeping mine over the years.

BIOLOGICAL DATA

Adult weight: 72-120 g.

Adult length: Head and body 14-19 cm, tail 10 cm.

Respiratory rate: 75 per minute (resting).

Body temperature: 38 degrees C when awake, a few degrees above the environmental temperature when in hibernation.

Life Span: Males – 4 years, though some may live to 8; females - 5 years, though there are records of some living to 12.

Reproduction: March to September, with peaks in April/May and July/August.

Oestrous cycle: Usually 13-14 days; range – 11-21.

Gestation: Usually 31-32 days; range – 28-35.

Emergence of young from nest box: About 35 days; range – 30-38 days.

Weaning: One week after emergence.

Number of young: Usually 3-5; range – 1-8.